A Note to Parents

DK READERS is a compelling program for beginning readers, designed in conjunction with leading literacy experts, including Dr. Linda Gambrell, Distinguished Professor of Education at Clemson University. Dr. Gambrell has served as President of the National Reading Conference, the College Reading Association, and the International Reading Association.

Beautiful illustrations and superb full-color photographs combine with engaging, easy-to-read stories to offer a fresh approach to each subject in the series. Each DK READER is guaranteed to capture a child's interest while developing his or her reading skills, general knowledge, and love of reading.

The five levels of DK READERS are aimed at different reading abilities, enabling you to choose the books that are exactly right for your child:

Pre-level 1: Learning to read
Level 1: Beginning to read
Level 2: Beginning to read alone
Level 3: Reading alone
Level 4: Proficient readers

The "normal" age at which a child begins to read can be anywhere from three to eight years old. Adult participation through the lower levels is very helpful for providing encouragement, discussing storylines, and sounding out unfamiliar words.

No matter which level you select, you can be sure that you are helping your child learn to read, then read to learn!

LONDON, NEW YORK, MUNICH,
MELBOURNE, and DELHI

Senior Editor Helen Murray
Designer Lauren Rosier
Jacket Designer Lauren Rosier
Design Manager Ron Stobbart
Publishing Manager Catherine Saunders
Art Director Lisa Lanzarini
Publisher Simon Beecroft
Publishing Director Alex Allan
Production Editor Andy Hilliard
Production Controller Melanie Mikellides
Reading Consultant Dr. Linda Gambrell

First published in the United States in 2012
by DK Publishing
375 Hudson Street
New York, New York 10014
10 9 8 7 6 5 4 3 2 1
LEGO and the LEGO logo are trademarks of the LEGO Group.
© 2012 the LEGO Group.
Produced by Dorling Kindersley
under license from the LEGO Group.

001—184098—July/12

DK books are available at special discounts when purchased in
bulk for sales promotions, premiums, fund-raising, or
educational use.
For details, contact:
DK Publishing Special Markets
375 Hudson Street
New York, New York 10014
SpecialSales@dk.com

A catalog record for this book is available
from the Library of Congress.

ISBN: 978-0-7566-9384-8 (Paperback)
ISBN: 978-0-7566-9385-5 (Hardcover)

Color reproduction by Media Development and Printing, UK
Printed and bound in the USA by Lake Book Manufacturing, Inc.

Discover more at
www.dk.com
www.LEGO.com

Contents

DK READERS

PROFICIENT
4
READERS

Welcome to Heartlake City

Written by Helen Murray

Heartlake City

Welcome to Heartlake City! There is always something fun and exciting to do here. You could explore the boutiques and cafés downtown, or enjoy an open-air concert in the park. Perhaps you might like to go to the pool to sunbathe and chat with friends, or catch a boat to Lighthouse Island to search for buried treasure? Anything is possible in Heartlake City.

Olivia

Emma

4

International sporting events and talent contests are held here, and if you are lucky, you might even catch a film crew shooting a movie!

The town is home to five smart, adventurous, and talented best friends: Emma, Mia, Stephanie, Andrea, and Olivia. They think Heartlake City is a wonderful place to live. Come and join the girls and explore their amazing home!

Emma
Fashionable Emma likes to explore the city's boutiques for cool clothes and accessories.

Stephanie

Andrea

Mia

Special offer
Hurry! There is
a great deal on
cupcakes at
the café today!

Sunny terrace
Andrea and
the girls like
to sit outside
on the terrace,
which overlooks
the beautiful
Lake Heart.

A fun place to work

Whether the girls are taking a road trip along the coast, shopping on Main Street, or planning an exciting event in the town, life is always fun in Heartlake City. For lucky Andrea, the fun doesn't stop when she is at her part-time job at the City Park Café. It is one of the coolest places to hang out in the city—and it is a great place to work, too!

The café is a central meeting spot for Olivia, Mia, Emma, Andrea, and Stephanie.

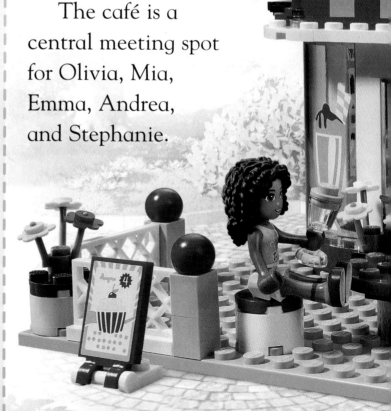

When Andrea is not working, she meets the girls to gossip over milkshakes and cupcakes.

Andrea works as a waitress at the busy café. Her first job of the day is to put out the sign that advertises the café's amazing cupcakes.

Dish of the day
As well as cakes, the café does a great range of delicious burgers and sandwiches.

Andrea works at the café with Marie, the owner. Marie is a great cook and a wonderful boss. For years, Marie's friends told her that she should open a café so the whole of Heartlake City could sample her food—so one day she did!

Marie bakes cakes and pies before the café opens. Her favorite moment of the day is when she pulls out a tasty cake from the oven. The wonderful smell that greets her makes all the hard work worthwhile.

The café stays busy all day. Andrea and Marie rush around taking orders and delivering tasty food to eager customers.

Andrea is an amazing singer and is always dreaming about becoming a pop star, even at work! Fortunately for Andrea, Marie encourages her to perform for customers at the café.

With Marie's fantastic baking and Andrea's incredible singing, the café draws in customers from all across Heartlake City!

Perfect pie
Marie bakes lots of different pies. The girls' favorite flavors are cherry, peach, and apple.

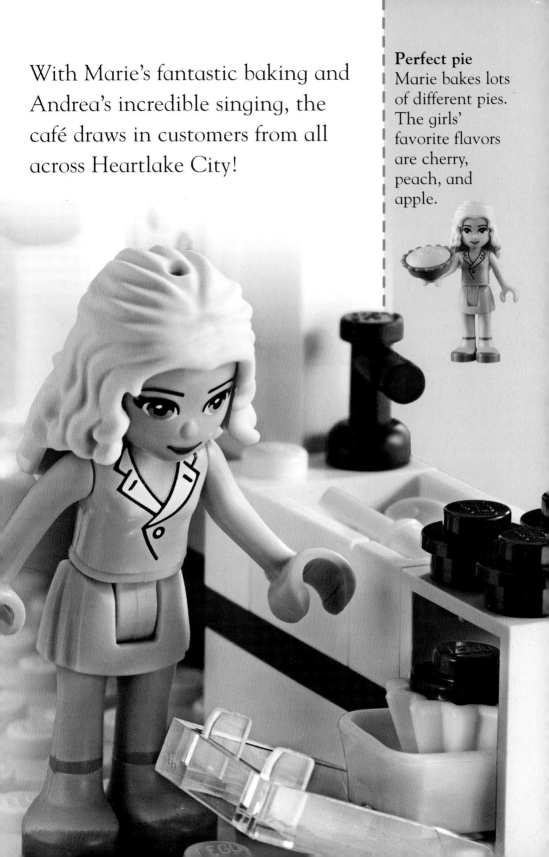

While washing the dishes, Marie plans which cakes and pies to bake in the morning. She decides on chocolate cupcakes and blueberry pie. Yum!

Andrea and Marie clean and tidy throughout the day, but they give the café a thorough clean once all the customers have gone home. Marie likes to make sure that the café is sparkling!

Bowl

Faucet

Cutlery

Oven

Andrea wipes down the booths and counters while Marie sweeps the floor and cleans the oven. There is a mountain of crumbs to wipe away! Marie jokes with Andrea that it is quicker if she sweeps the floor herself. Andrea spends as much time singing into the broom handle as she does sweeping!

There are always lots of dirty dishes, utensils, glasses, and baking trays to wash, but cheerful Marie doesn't mind. She is pleased because it means that there have been plenty of happy, well-fed customers.

Before they go home for the night, Marie and Andrea put everything back in its place, ready for another busy day at the City Park Café.

Today's takings
Marie counts up the money at the end of the day. It has been another successful day!

A spotless floor
Marie has high standards when it comes to cleanliness. She carefully sweeps up every last wrapper and crumb.

Time to relax

Heartlake City is a relaxed and laid-back place to live. Mia, Stephanie, Olivia, Andrea, and Emma like to take walks in the lush park, go for picnics in Clover Meadows, or set sail on a yacht on Lake Heart. But Emma's favorite place of all is the splash pool in her own back yard!

Emma the designer
Emma dreams of becoming a top fashion designer. She works hard designing and making new clothes, jewelry, and home furnishings at her cool design studio.

It is quiet and peaceful, with spectacular views of the beach. It really is the ultimate place to relax!

Emma likes to spend a lazy sunny afternoon cooling off in the pool and working on her tan. Sometimes she takes a quick nap on the lounger under the shade of the umbrella. She always makes sure she has a refreshing drink or ice-cream sundae close by.

Lush setting
Emma loves the calming scent of this pretty poolside plant.

Chic Emma
Emma is always stylish. The colors of her pool, lounger, and umbrella, go together perfectly.

Ice cream
The girls love to eat ice cream. Emma and Andrea like strawberry and vanilla best, Mia and Olivia like chocolate, and Stephanie's favorite flavor is cookie dough.

Emma, Andrea, Mia, Olivia, and Stephanie lead busy lives. Sometimes they need to take time out from schoolwork, hobbies, and part-time jobs, so Emma invites them over to spend a day in the sun. They have fun sunbathing and paddling in the pool.

The friends sing along to cool tunes on their MP3 players and relax on the sun loungers.

Sometimes Andrea helps Emma to make delicious ice-cream sundaes for all the girls. Andrea has learned some great tips from her part-time job at the City Park Café. She likes to add her own special touch with cherries, chocolate chips, and sprinkles on top. Yum!

Splash pool concert
Andrea loves to sing. She often gives her friends their own private poolside performance!

Olivia's family recently moved to Heartlake City. They live in the leafy Heartlake Heights area, which overlooks the beach and harbor.

Home sweet home

There's so much to see and do in Heartlake City, but sometimes there's no place like home. And Olivia's house is one of the coolest in the city. The girls like to head to Olivia's house to spend time together.

Bathroom

Roof terrace

Kitchen

Living room

Olivia, Andrea, Mia, Emma, and Stephanie have many choices about where to go in the beautiful house. They can watch movies in the comfortable living room, cook together in the spacious kitchen, and stargaze at night from the roof terrace.

The friends also enjoy spending time with Olivia's parents. Anna and Peter are always there with a sympathetic ear whenever the girls have any worries.

Olivia's bedroom

Swing

Baked treats
Olivia's mom bakes cakes for the girls. Fellow baker Stephanie loves to swap recipes and tips with her.

Olivia's workshop
Olivia loves science. She has a workshop where she goes to experiment and invent.

Prizes
Between them,
the girls have
won countless
trophies and
prizes for their
horseback riding
skills. Olivia has
proudly stuck her
latest award on
her wall.

Olivia, Emma, Mia, Stephanie, and Andrea often head upstairs to Olivia's bedroom. Emma decorated the room for Olivia when she first moved in. Doesn't it look beautiful?

The girls listen to music and give each other makeovers. They all crowd in front of the beautiful lighted mirror to try out new hairstyles. Sometimes they stay for sleepovers, too. Three of the girls squeeze into the bed while the other two sleep on the floor!

Diary

The girls often stay up late talking and don't always get as much sleep as they should!

Olivia loves it when her friends come to stay, but she also enjoys some quiet time once they have left. She writes about her friends, their dreams, and their adventures in her diary.

Olivia's cat
Missy is very playful. Her favorite game is hide-and-seek. But it looks like Olivia has discovered Missy a little too easily this time—she is in the bathroom!

Lights

Mirror

Perfume

Dressing table

19

Handy girl
Olivia can fix anything! She mended and repainted the mailbox when her family first moved to the house.

Olivia often invites her friends to barbecues in her beautiful front yard. Olivia's dad loves to cook outside. He grills sausages and chicken, which he coats in a delicious sauce. It is his secret recipe! Olivia's dad always makes sure he cooks something tasty for Mia, who doesn't eat meat—she is a vegetarian. He grills delicious vegetables, which he grows in his very own vegetable garden.

Olivia and her mom set up the table and chairs and bring plates, cutlery, and ketchup from the kitchen. The barbecue is ready!

Just opposite Olivia's house is a cool treehouse where the girls go to arrange parties, make top-secret plans, and camp out under the stars. They worked hard to fix and decorate the treehouse to make it a beautiful girls-only space.

The treehouse
The girls love to hang out at the treehouse in the summer. No boys and no parents are allowed!

Heartlake Vet

Heartlake City is not just a great place for people to live, it is a safe and caring place for animals, too. Heartlake Vet is where all the city's sick pets and wild animals go to be nursed back to health.

All kinds of animals, from birds and hedgehogs to dogs and horses, are cared for at this friendly, modern animal hospital.

Mailbox

Rescue
trolley

22

There are different areas for the animals to recover and get well again. Large animals can rest in a recovery stall, while small animals are looked after in a cage next door.

Sophie is Heartlake City's vet. She is gentle and kind to the animals and she works very hard. Animal-loving Mia volunteers part time at the vet. She is learning how to look after the different animals.

Mia
Mia is crazy about animals. She bonds naturally with animals and is practical and very hands-on. She would make a great vet.

Large animal stall

Patient sign

Faucet

Medicine

Small animal cage

23

Examination chart
Mia carefully records the patient's details on the chart.

The state-of-the-art surgery center is equipped with everything Sophie needs to work out what is wrong with the animals. Sophie gives each animal a thorough check-up on the examination table. Sometimes she takes an x-ray to check for broken bones or any other internal problems.

Feeding time
Mia feeds the animals twice a day. Some animals need to eat more than others!

Food trolley

There is a scale for monitoring the weights of each of the animals. Mia checks that the hedgehog is putting on weight. Fortunately, he is! He should be ready to be released back into the wild soon. There is also a heat lamp to warm up any poor animals that have been outside in the cold for a long time.

Aquarium
Sophie looks after Heartlake City's unwanted pet fish in this large tank. They are very pretty and colorful!

Aquarium

Phone

Reception desk

X-ray

Sink

Weighing scale

Heat lamp

25

Sophie soothes scared and timid animals with her soft voice and gentle nature.

Good hygiene
Sophie and Mia carefully clean all of the vet's tools in the sink after each use.

Sophie has all kinds of tools to monitor the animals' health and to make them feel better. She hangs a stethoscope around her neck, which she uses to listen to each animal's breathing and heartbeat. She also has a thermometer to monitor the animals' temperatures and a torch for checking their ears, too. Sophie gives the hedgehog some final checks before he can be released. She is pleased—his ears look nice and healthy!

The animal hospital is equipped with a huge variety of medicines to help each of the animals recover as quickly as possible. There are ice packs to soothe swelling and bruises and lots of bandages for broken bones and other injuries, too.

On the move
Sophie and Mia can quickly transport very sick or injured animals in the rescue trolley.

Emergency service
People call the surgery with emergencies. Sophie often rushes out of the door to visit sick pets at home.

Always prepared
Stephanie is super-organized. She always makes sure that there is plenty of food in the trailer for any rescued animals.

Always prepared
Stephanie is super-organized. She always makes sure that there is plenty of food in the trailer for any rescued animals.

Daisy
This mischievous little rabbit has a habit of wandering away from her bunny house.

Stephanie helps out Sophie, the vet, by patrolling Heartlake City looking for lost or wounded pets and wild animals. She rides around on a cool quad bike, called the Pet Patrol. The bike has big, sturdy wheels, which allow her to go off-road onto bumpy terrain. Stephanie attaches a trailer to the back of the quad bike, so there is a lot of space to carry rescued animals as well as food.

When Stephanie finds injured or sick animals, she delivers them to Sophie and Mia at Heartlake Vet. But if an animal is lost, she takes it home to its owner. Sociable Stephanie makes it her business to know everyone in the city, so she doesn't usually have any difficulties locating the pets' homes!

Stephanie has found Daisy, who disappeared from her bunny house. Luckily, she knows just where Daisy lives!

Dinner time
Daisy is happy to be back in her bunny house. Stephanie gives the hungry rabbit a tasty carrot.

Stable chic
Emma sometimes takes her love of design to the extreme. She once decorated hay with bows to add color to her horse's stable!

Riding camp
Stephanie, Mia, and Emma often go to summer riding camp. They have lots of fun while improving their riding skills.

Heartlake horses

One of the best things about Heartlake City is that there are lots of great places to go horseback riding. Well, that's what the girls think!

Mia, Emma, Andrea, Stephanie, and Olivia like to spend time at Heartlake Stables, which is located on the edge of Clover Meadows. They hone their riding and jumping skills at the stables. But for more exciting rides, they canter across the meadows and into the Whispering Woods.

Mia and Emma both have their own horses, Bella and Robin. All of the girls enjoy entering competitions, but Mia and Emma are the champion horseback riders of the group! They compete regularly in show jumping and dressage events across Heartlake City—and they usually win!

The horses at Heartlake Stables love to graze on the lush grass of Clover Meadows.

Mia's horse, Bella, lives at Heartlake Stables. Mia goes there every day to feed, groom, and ride Bella.

31

A girly day out

When Emma, Stephanie, Mia, Andrea, and Olivia want to treat themselves to a day of shopping and pampering, they head to Main Street.

People watching
Sometimes the girls need to rest their tired feet. They sit on their favorite bench and watch other shoppers pass by.

Beauty Shop

This chic shopping area is home to Heartlake City's trendiest shops, boutiques, and salons.

The girls' favorite place on Main Street is Butterfly Beauty Shop. They sometimes spend a whole afternoon trying out new looks and getting pampered.

Sarah, who works at the salon, is one of the coolest people the girls know. The girls like to ask Sarah for style tips and advice. Aspiring fashion designer Emma always listens especially closely!

Sarah is an amazing makeup artist. Girls come from all over Heartlake City to have their makeup done by Sarah. She helps them to find the perfect shades for their lips, cheeks, and eyes.

In the summer, Sarah offers makeovers on the street. Passers-by can't resist the hot new lipstick colors!

Make a wish
This upscale salon has a gorgeous fountain outside. The friends always make a wish as they toss a coin into the water.

Sarah
Sarah loves working at the salon. She hopes to open a salon of her very own one day.

Favorite lipstick
Emma spends time trying out all the different lipstick colors before finally settling on her favorite.

Makeup
Butterfly Beauty Shop stocks a fantastic range of makeup. It always has the season's hottest shades.

Sarah loves to advise Emma, Stephanie, Mia, Olivia, and Andrea on makeup. The girls have great fun trying out different looks before a special party or event. There is always so much choice—it is hard to know which colors to pick!

When schoolwork, part-time jobs, and hobbies take their toll, the girls relax with a pampering session in the salon. The friends take it in turns to rest in the comfy chair while Sarah styles their hair. She keeps a close eye on the runways and fashion magazines and enjoys trying out the latest looks on the girls! Sometimes Sarah paints the girls' nails, too. The five friends always leave the salon feeling refreshed and fabulous!

Emma and Sarah chat about fashion while Sarah styles Emma's hair.

Hairdresser

The girls go to the Butterfly Beauty Shop to have their hair cut and styled. Sarah is a fantastic hairdresser!

Stephanie, Olivia, Mia, Andrea, and Emma like to shop for clothes and accessories, too. Butterfly Beauty Shop sells a wide range of glamorous sunglasses, barrettes, and bows.

Natural talent
Emma is great at hunting down accessories to complement her friends' outfits.

Creative Emma loves to help her friends select new outfits and accessories. She always seems to know what will look just right. What will the girls buy today?

Emma is always on the lookout for design inspiration. A shopping day with her four best friends usually provides her with plenty of new ideas!

Treats
Mia gives the dogs bones to reward them for being so well behaved!

Charlie
Charlie has a light-colored coat, so Mia takes special care to get him sparkling clean.

Special events

One of the best things about living in Heartlake City is that there are always lots of fun and exciting events to go to. One of Mia's favorites is the annual Heartlake Dog Show. Mia loves to have the opportunity to put her animal training skills into action!

In the show's grooming area, Mia works hard preparing the puppies, Scarlett and Charlie, for the show.

Mia scrubs the dogs with a special dog shampoo and styles their hair. The dogs don't like getting wet, but they like it when Mia gently combs their hair. For the ultimate finishing touch, Mia dresses up each puppy with a pretty purple bow.

Grooming
Mia has everything she needs to pamper Scarlett and Charlie before their big moment on the dog show stage.

The bench
The dogs have to tread carefully as they walk along this narrow bench in the Most Agile Puppy event.

The dog show has a large obstacle course and runway where the dogs compete for prizes. There are lots of individual events in each show. This year, Charlie and Scarlett are competing for the Most Agile Puppy prize and the Cutest Puppy award. Could one of the puppies even win Best in Show?

Animal-lover Mia has a natural talent when it comes to training animals.

Grooming area

Seesaw

Charlie and Scarlett know exactly what to do in the obstacle course because Mia has taught them so well. They are sure to win a prize!

The runway
Scarlett and Charlie excitedly parade down the runway as they compete for the Cutest Puppy award.

Light

Camera

Runway

Official photographer
Emma takes some great shots of the happy winners.

Pretty in pink
Mia gives the puppies new pink bows to reward them for all their hard work.

Charlie and Scarlett have done it! They have won first and second place in the Most Agile Puppy event. They completed the obstacle course in the fastest times and with no mistakes. All Mia's training has paid off! Mia can hear Olivia, Stephanie, Emma, and Andrea, cheering loudly in the audience. It has been a wonderful day!

The puppies stand proudly on the winners' podium while Mia excitedly gives them their awards. They have won so many ribbons that soon Mia will need to find a new place for all of the prizes!

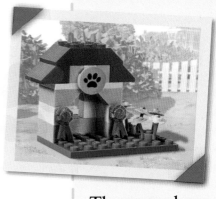

The puppy house
Mia sticks the ribbons onto the puppy house and puts the dogs to bed. The puppies will need lots of sleep after an exciting but tiring day.

A born performer

Although music is her real passion, Andrea loves to dance and act, too.

The stage

Standing under the spotlights of the open-air stage, Andrea feels like a superstar!

Of all the cool things happening in Heartlake City, the girls look forward to Andrea performing on stage the most. People come from all over the city to listen to Andrea sing at an open-air concert in the park. Andrea delights the audience with her amazing talent and beautiful voice. The concert reminds Stephanie, Emma, Mia, and Olivia just how lucky they are to have such a talented singer as their best friend.

Andrea has her sights set on stardom. She dreams of being spotted by a talent scout from a record label. Could today be her lucky day?

Andrea steps in front of the curtain to greet her friends and fans. She is becoming the biggest star in Heartlake City!

Songwriter
Andrea writes music at her grand piano. Performing and composing is thirsty work, so she makes sure she always has a glass of water close by.

Outdoors-loving Olivia

Olivia is always prepared for adventure. She would never leave the house without a map or compass!

Adventure all around

The girls all share a sense of adventure. But nobody loves to plan a trip more than Stephanie, the chief organizer of the group.

The friends often hit the road in Stephanie's stylish convertible. They drive beyond the suburbs and busy downtown area of Heartlake City to the Whispering Woods and Clearspring Mountains.

Traveling companion

Sometimes Stephanie's cute dog Coco is lucky enough to come along for the ride.

The girls hike the mountain trails to see amazing views of the city below. They also like to explore the woods, looking out for wildlife. So far, they have seen deer, rabbits, moles, and beautiful butterflies. There is a rumor that bears have been spotted deep inside the woods, but the friends haven't explored that far—yet!

There are still so many exciting adventures to plan in Heartlake City. Where will the five friends go next?

Musical Andrea
Andrea provides cool music for the journey—and she always sings along!

Caring Mia
Mia once brought a sick rabbit home from the woods and nursed him back to health.

Quiz

1. What is Andrea's first job of the day at the City Park Café?

2. At barbecues, why does Olivia's dad cook different meals for Mia?

3. What instrument does the vet use to listen to an animal's breathing and heartbeat?

4. What did Emma once do to decorate her horse's stable?

5. Which event did Charlie and Scarlett win at Heartlake Dog Show?

1. She puts out the sign that advertises cupcakes, 2. Because Mia is a vegetarian, 3. A stethoscope, 4. She decorated the hay with bows, 5. The Most Agile Puppy event